OUR SPACE

Revealing the unknown world of facts!

BPI INDIA PVT LTD

Introduction

Space is the vast expanse that includes the universe and all its components. It is the totality of everything that exists, including all physical matter and energy. Since ancient times, the universe has attracted the attention of astronomers and ordinary people alike. With the development of technology, man has even reached space and landed on moon.

'Our Space' imparts information about everything that is a part of space. Beginning with the origin of the universe, the book includes information about its expansion, the formation of planets and other celestial bodies, the phenomena that occur in space, space shuttles and humans in space. Young learners will get answers to all their queries related to space and its components. The book is packed with colourful illustrations and relevant information to make it an interesting read for children.

ISBN : 978817693877-8

Published by

BPI INDIA PVT LTD
F-213/A, Ground Floor, Old Mehrauli Badarpur Road,
Lado Sarai, New Delhi- 110030 (India)
Tel: +91-11-43394300-99
e-mail: sales@bpiindia.com

Contents

Universe

The universe includes all matter and energy that exists. It includes the Earth and all the other planets, stars, galaxies and all that they contain. The entire cosmos, from the smallest particles on Earth, to the longest galaxies in space is the Universe.

Colour of Our Universe

The colour of the Universe was identified by astronomers at the John Hopkins University, USA. At first, the colour was thought to be greenish-white but later it was confirmed as beige.

Composition

The Universe is composed of dark energy and dark matter. It consists of 73 per cent dark energy and 23 per cent dark matter. The remaining 4 per cent consists of atoms.

The Space

Observe

Look at the colour of the sky in the morning and compare it with the colour of the sky at night.

Elemental Composition

The elemental composition of the Universe is around 78 per cent hydrogen and 20 per cent helium. The remaining one per cent is composed of other chemical elements.

Cosmology

Cosmology is the scientific study of the origin, development and future of the Universe. It also deals with physical and metaphysical means of sustenance of the Universe.

Milky Way

Cosmology

The word cosmology is derived from 'cosmos' meaning universe and 'logy' meaning study.

Various Planets

Multiverse

Multiverse is a hypothetical set of multiple possible universes. It includes our Universe along with everything that exists. The different universes within a multiverse are called parallel universes.

Observable Universe

Observable universe is a part of the Universe, which can be seen with the help of large telescopes. It has around 140 billion galaxies made up of billions of stars. According to inflationary cosmology, the observable universe is much smaller than the entire Universe.

Dark Matter

Astronomers believe that 95 per cent of the mass of the Universe consists of dark matter. Dark matter is not visible to us because it emits no radiation and can be detected only by its gravitational pull on visible matter.

A Part of the Universe

Origin of the Universe

The Universe was created during a cosmic explosion called the Big Bang that occurred between 10 to 20 billion years ago. Before the Big Bang, all matter that exists in the present day Universe was condensed into a tiny area. After the explosion, the matter scattered as dust, cloud or mist all around.

Big Bang Explosion

Big Bang Theory

In 1927, Georges Lemaitre, a Belgian mathematician and Catholic priest, first proposed that the Universe had originated from the Big Bang explosion. In 1929, Edwin Hubble was the first to observe that the Universe was continuously expanding. This observation provided the foundation for the Big Bang Theory.

Age of the Universe

The age of the Universe refers to the time that has elapsed since the Big Bang explosion.

Steady-State Theory

The Steady-State theory fills the gaps left in the Big Bang Theory. Fred Hoyle, Hermann Bondi and Thomas Gold proposed the Steady-State Theory in 1948. The theory states that matter is being created continuously at the rate of hundreds of atoms per year. It also states that although the universe is expanding, its appearance and density does not change.

Fred Hoyle

Pulsating Theory

The Pulsating theory states that the universe is pulsating or expanding and contracting alternately. According to this theory, the current expansion of the universe will stop at a certain point of time by gravitational pull. Once the expansion stops, it will start contracting again. After contracting to a certain size, an explosion will occur and the universe will start expanding again.

Orion - A Constellation

Constellations

A constellation is a group of stars that are connected to each other to make a figure. There are 88 constellations in the sky. All the 88 constellations are not visible throughout the year. Some can only be seen during certain seasons depending on the Earth's annual revolution around the Sun.

Look

Look at the sky at night and look for a pattern of stars that resembles a figure.

Naming a Constellation

Most constellations were named in Greek and Latin by the ancient Greeks and the Romans. Ptolemy, the great astronomer from Egypt, named 48 of the 50 constellations known during his time. The constellations were generally named after animals and mythological characters.

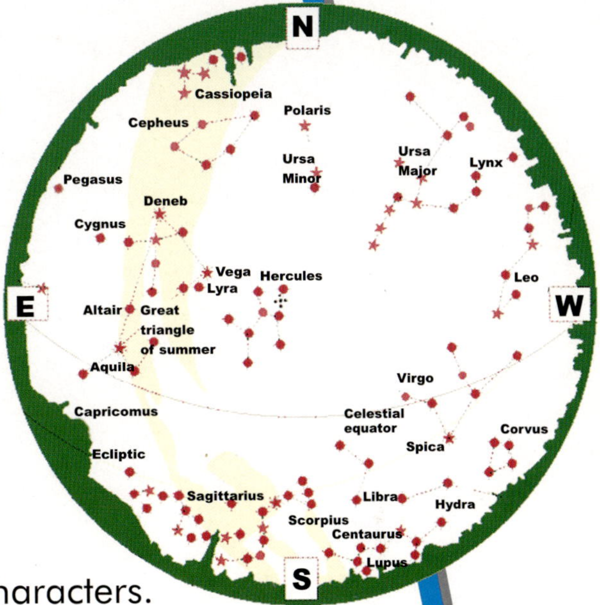

Constellation Map

Names of Constellations

Constellations have fascinated human beings over the ages. Some of the famous constellations are Orion, Leo, Ursa Major, Ursa Minor and Crux.

Constellations of the Zodiac

Every year, the Sun passes through an imaginary ring of 12 constellations. This ring of constellations is known as the Zodiac. Ptolemy named the constellations of the Zodiac in the 2nd century BC.

Stars in the Sky

Stars

Stars are extremely large gaseous bodies found in the Universe. They produce enormous amounts of light and other forms of energy through nuclear fusion. The Sun is the star closest to the Earth.

Binary Stars

Binary stars are a pair of stars that move around a common centre of mass. They are also known as double stars.

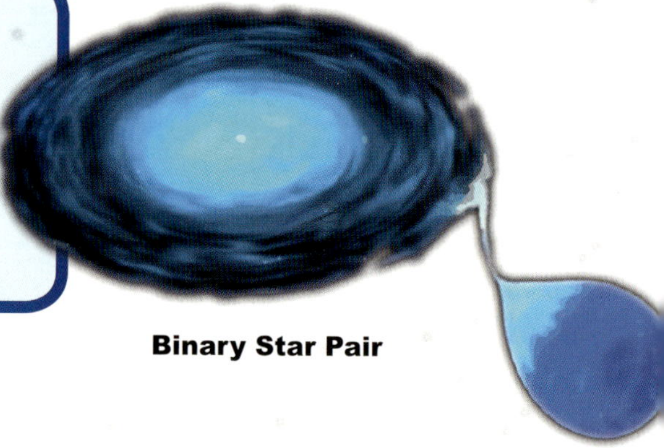

Binary Star Pair

Birth of Stars

Stars are born from huge clouds of dust and hydrogen, helium and traces of other heavier elements. These clouds collapse under gravitational forces and the gravitational attraction between the atoms increases which adds more atoms to the centre. Finally, the centre gets hotter and the star begins to shine.

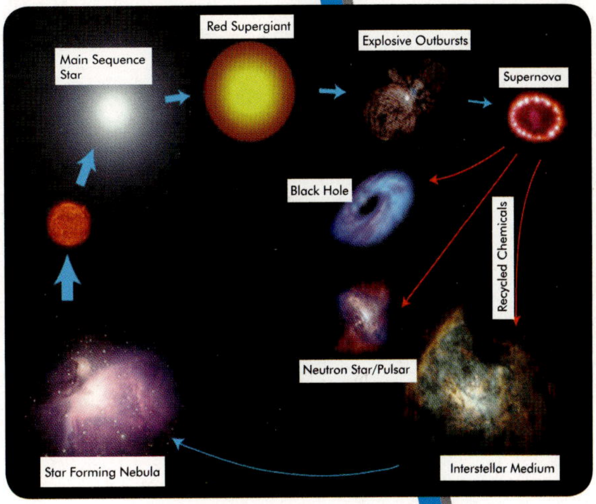

Life Cycle of a Star

Size of the Stars

Stars vary in their shape and size. The neutron stars have a radius of only about 10 kilometres, while the Pistol Star is 100 times bigger than the Sun.

Variable Stars

Some stars keep on changing their brightness. Such stars are known as variable stars. Intrinsic and extrinsic variable stars are the two types of variable stars. Intrinsic variable stars change in brightness because of the change in their physical properties. Extrinsic variable stars change in brightness because of external properties, such as rotation or eclipses.

White Dwarfs

White dwarfs are dying stars that emit a white glow. Most white dwarfs are formed after a red giant has burned all its original hydrogen and helium. Such stars expel most of their outer material creating a planetary nebula. The hot core keeps glowing until it cools down, which takes almost a billion years or so.

Neutron Stars

Neutron stars are very dense stars composed of neutrons. Neutron stars are the endpoint stars, which are four to eight times as massive as the Sun. When these huge stars finish burning their nuclear fuel, they undergo a supernova explosion. This explosion blows off the outer layers of the star and the central region collapses under gravity.

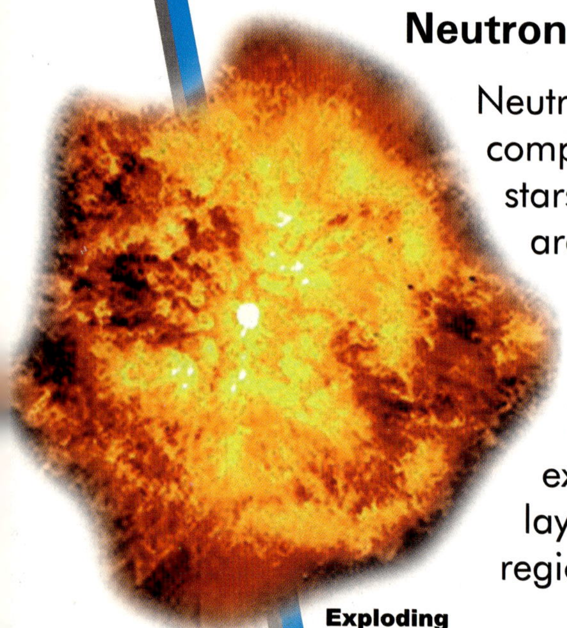

Exploding Supernova

Nebula

Nebula is a cloud of dust particles and gases in space. Nebulae are among the most beautiful objects in the universe. A nebula is composed of about 90 per cent hydrogen, 10 per cent helium and 0.1 per cent heavy elements. Nebulae are divided into emission nebulae, reflection nebulae, dark nebulae, planetary nebulae and supernova remnants.

Emission Nebula

An emission nebula is a nebula that glows and emits reddish light. The reddish light is emitted when electrons and protons combine to form hydrogen. Emission nebulae are among the most beautiful objects in the sky. The Orion Nebula is an emission nebula.

Horsehead Nebula in Orion

Dark Nebula

A dark nebula blocks all light from objects behind it. Dark nebulae do not have a defined regular shape and are very similar to reflection nebulae in composition. They are usually seen together with emission and reflection nebulae.

Crab Nebula

The Crab Nebula is the remnant of a supernova that exploded in 1054 AD. The nebula is located in the constellation Taurus and is around 6,500 light years away from Earth. The nebula was first observed in 1731 by John Bevis.

Crab Nebula

Planetary Nebula

Planetary nebulae are nebulae that look like planets because of their round shape. A planetary nebula surrounds a star. Planetary nebulae are formed by the gases released during the explosion of an extremely hot star. The Ring Nebula (M57) in the constellation Lyra is an example of a planetary nebula.

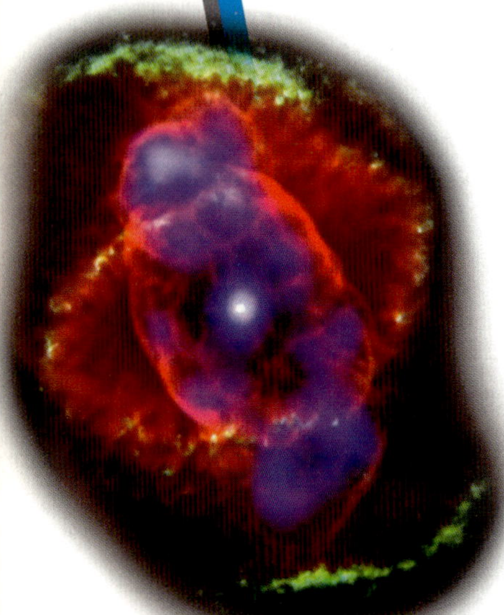

Planetary Nebula

Black Hole

A black hole is the remnant of a super collapsed star. The gravitational force of a black hole is so strong that nothing can escape it, not even light. Because no light escapes the star, it is called a black hole. The concept of black holes was proposed by Albert Einstein in his Theory of General Relativity in 1915.

Black Hole

Formation of Black Holes

Black holes are formed when stars, more than three times the mass of the sun, die out. They are formed when all the hydrogen of a dying star is exhausted and nuclear fusion stops and gravitation takes over. As gravitation dominates, the star starts to collapse and results in the formation of a black hole.

Wormhole

A wormhole is a hypothetical tunnel in space-time that might connect two black holes. Scientists believe that wormholes can have both ends at two different ends of the Universe or one end emerging in another time or Universe.

Super Massive Black Holes

Super massive black holes are formed from many smaller black holes. They are of several billion solar masses. Almost all galaxies have a super massive black hole at their centre.

Super Massive Black Holes

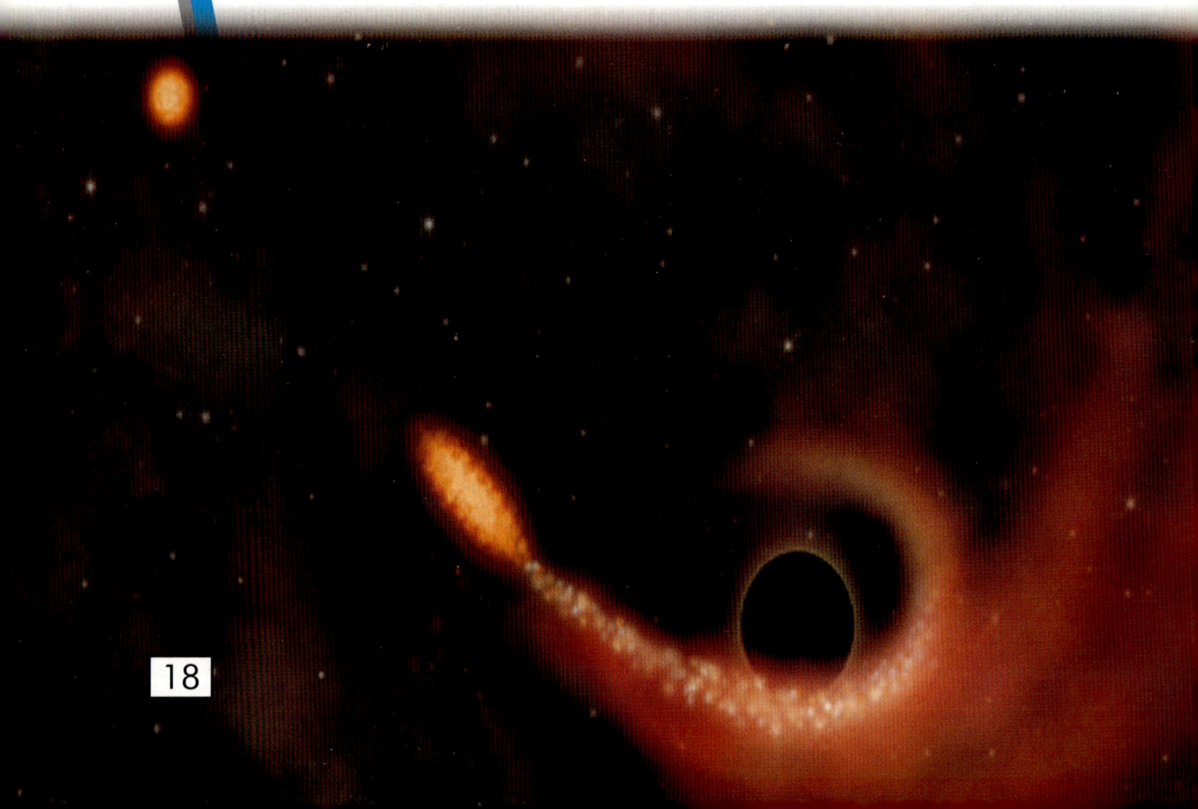

Galaxy

A galaxy is a huge collection of gravitationally bound stars, dust and gas. It is believed that more than 100 billion galaxies are scattered throughout the Universe. A galaxy may contain star systems, star clusters and various intersteller clouds. Dark matter, an important part of a galaxy, accounts for around 90 per cent of the mass of a galaxy.

Clusters

Galaxies are found in groups known as clusters. Clusters generally consist of 50 to 1000 galaxies. Our galaxy, the Milky Way, belongs to the cluster Local Group. Various clusters and groups of galaxies together form superclusters.

Galaxy Cluster

Spiral Galaxy

Different Shapes of Galaxies

There are three types of galaxies. Elliptical galaxies are shaped like an ellipse. Spiral galaxies are galaxies that resemble a disc and irregular galaxies are neither elliptical nor spiral. They have little symmetry in their structure.

Find

Find out one name each of the three kinds of galaxies.

Dwarf Galaxies

Dwarf galaxies are tiny galaxies. They are about one-hundredth the size of the Milky Way. These galaxies contain only a few billion stars. They too can be classified as elliptical, spiral or irregular.

Milky Way

The Milky Way galaxy is home to our solar system. The Milky Way is a spiral galaxy and has about 200 billion stars. All objects in the galaxy orbit around a common centre of mass. This centre of mass is called the galactic centre.

Milky Way Galaxy

Spiral Galaxies

Spiral galaxies are galaxies that resemble a disk. They have a central nucleus with spiral arms extending outwards. The arms have many hot, young, blue and blue-white stars and are regions of active star formation. The stars make the arms easily visible. Most spiral galaxies are made up of middle-aged stars. The M100 galaxy in the Virgo Cluster is an example of a spiral galaxy.

Age of Our Milky Way

The Milky Way is one of the oldest galaxies. Scientists believe that it is around 13.6 billion years old.

Local Group

The Milky Way is a member of the Local Group of galaxies. The group was first recognised by the Hubble space telescope. There are over 30 members in the Local Group.

Arms of the Milky Way

Arms of the Milky Way

The major arms of the Milky Way galaxy are the Perseus Arm, Sagittarius Arm, Centaurus Arm and Cygnus Arm. Our solar system is in a minor arm called the Orion Spur. The arms are named after the constellations seen in their direction.

Our Solar System

Our solar system comprises a group of celestial objects located in the Milky Way galaxy. It is made up of eight planets, their moons, dwarf planets, asteroids and meteoroids and several other smaller celestial bodies.

Solar System

Inner Solar System

The inner solar system refers to the region comprising the inner planets, i.e., Mercury, Venus, Earth and Mars, alongwith the asteriods. These objects are relatively close to the Sun and are composed mainly of silicates and metals.

Inner Solar System

Outer Solar System

The outer solar system refers to the region comprising the outer planets, i.e. Jupiter, Saturn, Uranus and Neptune and their large moons. This region also includes many comets. These objects are far away from the Sun and are composed mainly of water, ammonia and methane.

Outer Solar System

Did You Know?

Astronomers believe that the solar system is around 4.5 billion years old.

Other Solar Systems

There exist many other solar systems like our own solar system. These solar systems can be detected by measuring the gravitational pull of the planets on the star they orbit. Astronomers measure this gravitational pull and use it to calculate the orbit and mass of the planet. Till now astronomers have been able to find around 70 other solar systems.

Sun

The Sun is the largest and the most important object in the solar system. It is the main source of light, heat and other forms of energy on Earth. Without the Sun, there would be no life on Earth. The Sun is the largest and the only star in our solar system.

Sun

Corona

The corona is the hottest part of the Sun's atmosphere. The temperature in this layer can reach really high up to about 111,109,333°C during solar flares.

Age of the Sun

Scientists believe that the Sun is about 4.5 billion years old and will continue to burn fuel for the next 5 billion years.

Core of the Sun

The core forms the central region of the Sun. It is primarily made up of hydrogen and helium and contains almost half the Sun's mass. Almost all the fusion reactions in the Sun take place in the core. These reactions emit a lot of energy that lights up the surface and makes it a very hot place. The temperature at the core is about 15,000,000°C.

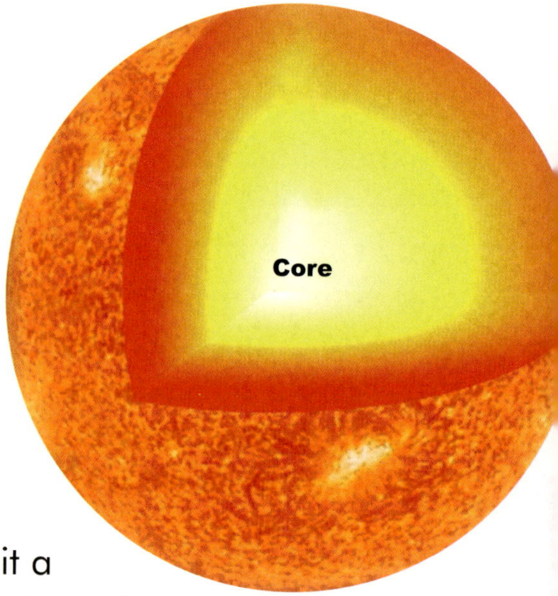

Sun and Its Interior

Spotty Sun

Sunspots are cool areas on the Sun that appear as dark patches. They are formed when the radiation of heat in some areas on the Sun becomes less because of the Sun's magnetic fields. Sunspots increase in number every 11 years.

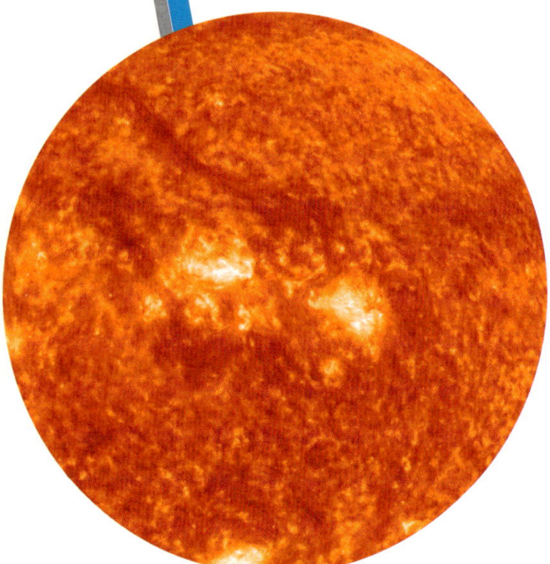

Sunspots

Planets

A planet is a celestial body that orbits the Sun or any other star. Our solar system consists of eight major planets. They are Mercury, Venus, Earth, Mars, Jupiter, Saturn, Uranus and Neptune. These planets vary greatly in mass, temperature and the rate of rotation.

Dwarf Planet

Dwarf Planet

In the year 2006, the International Astronomical Union (IAU) adopted the term dwarf planet to classify a celestial body that like all other planets orbits the Sun but has not cleared the neighbourhood around its orbit. By this definition Pluto was classified as a dwarf planet.

Minor Planets

Minor planets are small objects found in the solar system whose orbits lie between the Sun and the asteroid belt. These objects are larger than meteoroids but smaller than planets and therefore are not considered as planets.

Mercury

Mercury is the closest planet to the Sun. It is the smallest planet of the solar system. Mercury orbits the Sun faster than any other planet. It is the second densest planet after Earth. It takes around 88 Earth days to complete one revolution. A day on Mercury is 58.6 Earth days long.

Mercury

Learn

"My Very Elegant Mother Just Served Us Noodles".

The first letter in these words is also the first letter of the planets in their order. Now, can you remember the names?

Atmosphere of Mercury

Mercury does not have an atmosphere. The temperature on the surface reaches to a maximum of 430°C during the day. Nights are extremely cold as the planet fails to retain any heat. Night temperature drops to a minimum of -170°C on the planet.

Surface Features of Mercury

The surface of Mercury is quite similar to the surface of the Earth's Moon. It is made up of rocks and metals and is full of impact craters. With a diameter of about 4,828 kilometres, the planet is barely larger than the Earth's Moon.

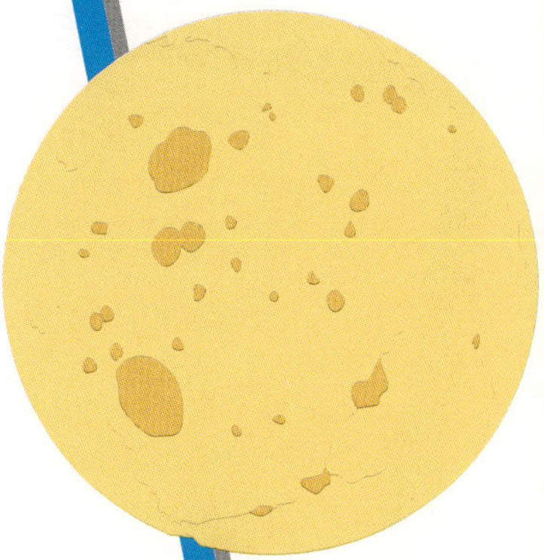

Surface of Mercury

Surface of Moon

Caloris Basin

Caloris Basin is the largest crater on Mercury. It has a diameter of around 1,481.6 kilometres and is surrounded by a ring of mountains. The crater was formed by the impact of a large meteorite. The floor of the crater is filled with lava plains.

Mission MESSENGER

NASA's Space Environment, GEochemistry and Ranging (MESSENGER) is the first spacecraft to orbit the planet Mercury. The spacecraft was launched in 2004. MESSENGER is supposed to orbit the planet and study its surface, crust and atmosphere. The spacecraft completed its flyby of Venus and left for Mercury on June 5, 2007.

MESSENGER on Its Way to Mercury

Various Names of Mercury

The planet Mercury has been known by various names over the ages. The Greeks named it Apollo and Hermes. The planet was named Mercury by the Romans after their winged messenger of gods.

Venus

Venus is the second planet from the Sun. It is the third-smallest planet in the solar system with a diameter of about 7,519 kilometres. The planet takes around 225 Earth days to orbit the Sun. A day on Venus is 243 Earth days long. Venus is the brightest object in the sky after the Sun and the Moon. It is known as both 'morning star' and 'evening star' as it can be seen shining brightly before sunrise and after sunset.

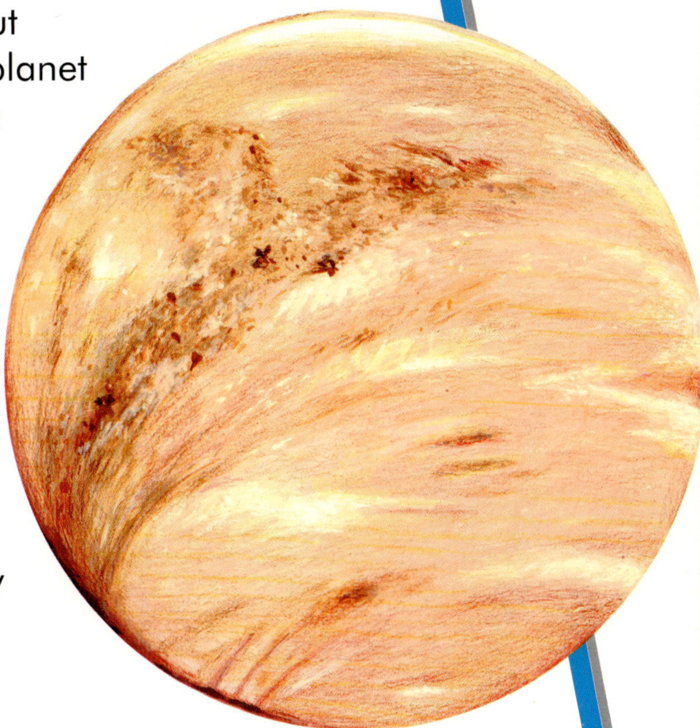

Venus

Atmosphere of Venus

Venus has a dense atmosphere. It is 90 times heavier than the Earth's atmosphere. The thick atmosphere traps most of the Sun's heat. The surface temperature of the planet remains around 470°C making it the hottest planet in our solar system.

Surface Features of Venus

Venus has a hot and dry surface. Most of the planet is covered with flat and smooth plains. The planet also has level grounds, mountains, canyons and valleys. Around 35 per cent of the surface area of the planet is covered by mountainous regions.

Earth's Twin

Venus is often called Earth's twin because of the similarity in shape, size and composition.

Earth

Earth is our home planet. It is the third planet from the Sun. It has a diameter of about 12,682 kilometres at the equator and 12,640 kilometres at the poles. The planet moves around the Sun in about 365 days, 6 hours and 9 minutes. The length of a day on Earth is approximately 23 hours, 56 minutes.

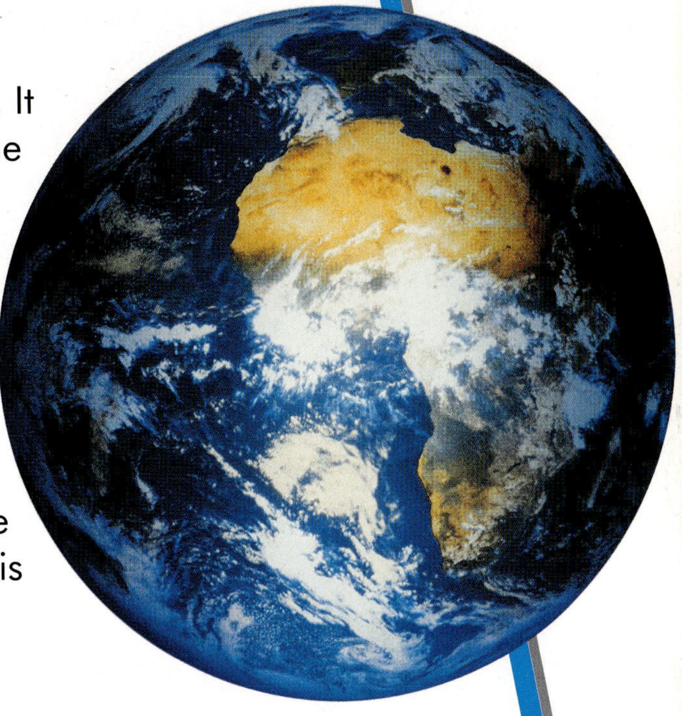

Earth

Formation of the Earth

When the Sun was formed about 5,000 million years ago, large clouds of dust and gases were released. This cosmic dust and gases condensed to form the Earth.

Atmosphere of the Earth

Earth is covered by a thin atmosphere composed of nitrogen (78 per cent), oxygen (21 per cent) and other gases (1 per cent). The atmosphere is divided into four layers—troposphere, stratosphere, mesosphere and ionosphere. The atmosphere scatters blue light and fills the sky with the colour blue. This makes our planet appear blue when seen from space.

Surface of the Earth

Earth has the most varied surface of all the planets in the solar system. The poles are covered with vast glaciers of ice whereas arid deserts are found near the equator. It also has large areas of land dominated by plants and trees and large areas covered with water.

Shape of the Earth

The shape of the Earth is not a perfect sphere. It is called a geoid. The planet is flattened at the poles and bulges at the equator.

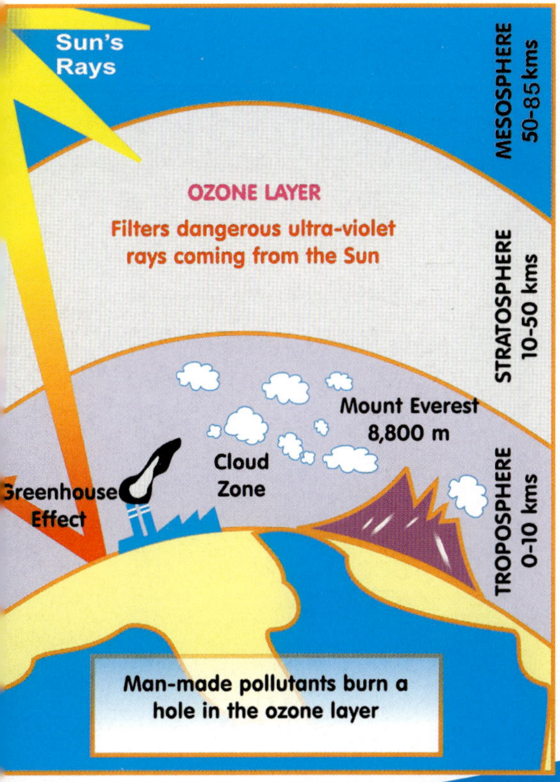

Ozone Layer

The ozone layer is a layer of ozone gas that is present in our atmosphere. It protects the Earth from harmful ultraviolet radiations.

The Ozone Layer

Earth as a Unique Planet

Earth is the only planet in our solar system that harbours life. It is home to all known life in the Universe. Animals, plants and other organisms are found almost everywhere on the Earth. Earth's optimum distance from the Sun provides it with the right amount of warmth and light for life to survive. The presence of water on the planet also helps support life.

Water on Earth

The Earth is the only planet that has an abundance of liquid water on its surface. Almost 70 per cent of the planet is covered with water. But only a small portion of the water is suitable for drinking. About 97 per cent of the water found on Earth is the salty water of the oceans. Much of the fresh water is frozen in the polar ice caps.

Surface of Earth

Inside the Earth

The interior of the Earth is divided into four layers. The crust is the outermost layer and the mantle lies just below the crust. The innermost part is the core. The core is divided into the inner and outer core.

Aryabhatta

Aryabhatta was a brilliant Indian mathematician-astronomer of the 5th century A.D. He accurately predicted that the Earth was spherical in shape. He also stated that the Earth rotated on its own axis.

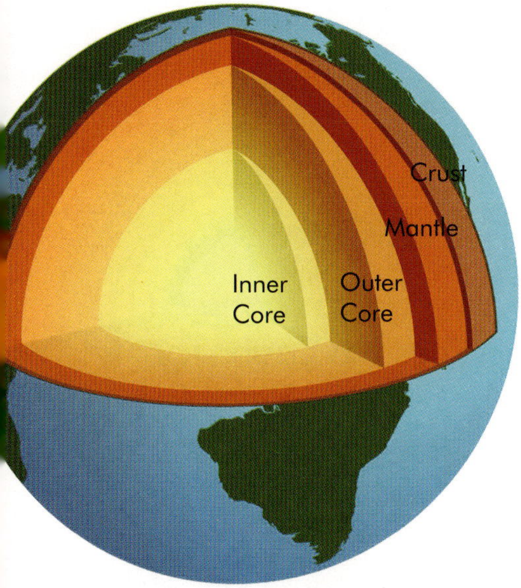

Interior of the Earth

Core, Mantle and Crust

The crust is the thin, outermost layer. The layer that extends below the Earth's crust is the mantle and the innermost layer of the Earth is the core. The inner core is a solid metal core while the outer core is a liquid molten core composed of nickel and iron.

Moon

Moon is Earth's only natural satellite. It is the second brightest object in the sky after the Sun. The Moon too was formed about 4.6 billion years ago. It is much smaller than the Earth. It is also much less massive than Earth. The moon is at a distance of about 3,82,168 kilometres from the Earth. It takes around 29½ days to complete one rotation on its axis and takes around 23¹/₃ days to complete one revolution around the Earth.

Phases of the Moon

Phases of the Moon

The Moon appears to change its shape as it orbits the Earth. The different shapes are known as the phases of the Moon. The Moon goes through four phases in one lunar month or 29½ Earth days. The four phases of the Moon are new moon, first quarter, full moon and the last quarter.

Surface Features of Moon

The great Italian astronomer Galileo Galilei was the first to study and map the Moon's surface in 1609. Galileo used a telescope to make his observations. He found that the Moon had hills and plains. Most of the craters were formed by the impact of meteoroids, asteroids and comets. It has shallow depressions called 'basins' and broad flat plains known as 'maria'.

Surface of the Moon

> **Did You Know?**
>
> The surface of the Moon is covered with a powdery dust called 'regolith'.

Moon and Water

Moon and Tides

Tides are the regular rising and falling of the ocean's surface. They are primarily caused by the gravitational pull of the Moon and Sun. The Moon's gravity pulls at the Earth causing the oceans to bulge out in the direction of the Moon. English scientist, Sir Isaac Newton, was the first to explain tides.

Craters on the Moon

Moon's craters are formed by the impact of meteoroids, asteroids and comets. Craters on the moon are named after famous scientists. The Copernicus Crater is named after Nicolaus Copernicus, a Polish astronomer. The Archimedes Crater is named after the Greek mathematician Archimedes.

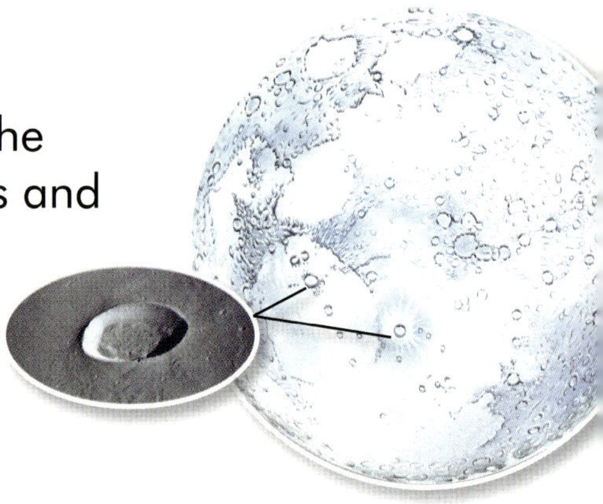

Craters

Visits to the Moon

Apollo 11 Landing on Moon

The first visit to the Moon was made by the Soviet spacecraft Luna 1 in 1959. In the same year, the Soviet spacecraft Luna 2 made its impact on the surface of the Moon. In 1966, Luna 9 made the first successful lunar soft landing and Luna 10 was the first unmanned vehicle to orbit the moon. The Apollo 11 was the first spacecraft to land people successfully on the moon in 1969. Neil Armstrong became the first man to set foot on the moon.

Mars

Mars is a terrestrial planet like Earth, Mercury and Venus. It is made up of three layers- the core, mantle and crust. It is the second smallest planet in the solar system with a diameter of about 6,794.650 kilometres. The planet takes around 687 Earth days to complete one revolution around the Sun. The length of a day on Mars is 24 hours, 39 minutes and 35 seconds.

Mars

Atmosphere of Mars

Mars has a thin atmosphere. It is mainly composed of carbon dioxide (95.3 per cent). Nitrogen, argon, carbon monoxide, water vapour and a small amount of oxygen are also found in the atmosphere of Mars.

Surface Features of Mars

Mars has a cratered surface. It is covered with fine-grained reddish dust. The surface in the southern hemisphere is old and heavily cratered. The northern hemisphere has few craters and the surface has been smoothened by repeated lava flows from several volcanoes that erupted in this hemisphere.

Red Planet

Mars is said to be a 'Red Planet' because of its appearance as seen from the Earth.

Red Planet

Climate on Mars

Mars too has seasonal changes like the Earth. But given its distance from the Sun, seasons on Mars are quite cold. Temperatures rarely rise above the freezing point. The planet also experiences huge duststorms blowing across it.

Moons of Mars

Mars has two moons: Phobos and Deimos. They were discovered by Asaph Hall in 1877. Phobos is larger than Deimos. Both the moons have a heavily cratered surface. They are covered with dust and loose rocks.

Volcanoes

Mars has many volcanoes. The largest volcano in the solar system, Olympus Mons, is on Mars. The volcano is almost 27 kilometres high.

Surface of Mars

Jupiter

Jupiter is the largest planet in the solar system. The planet is about 300 times more massive than the Earth. It is the fifth planet from the Sun and is around 7,74,04,954 kilometres away from it. The planet takes about 12 Earth years to orbit the Sun and completes one rotation in about 10 hours.

Jupiter

Atmosphere of Jupiter

Jupiter is a giant ball of gas with little or no surface. Its atmosphere is mostly made up of molecular hydrogen (87 per cent) and helium (14 per cent). Other substances present are methane, ammonia and phosphine.

Surface of Jupiter

Jupiter is a giant gas ball. It, therefore, has little or no surface. The planet has visible clouds of ammonia. Jupiter may have a solid and rocky core surrounded by liquid gases. Water also exists on the planet. The dark belts and light zones of the planet are formed by the strong winds that blow in the upper atmosphere of the planet.

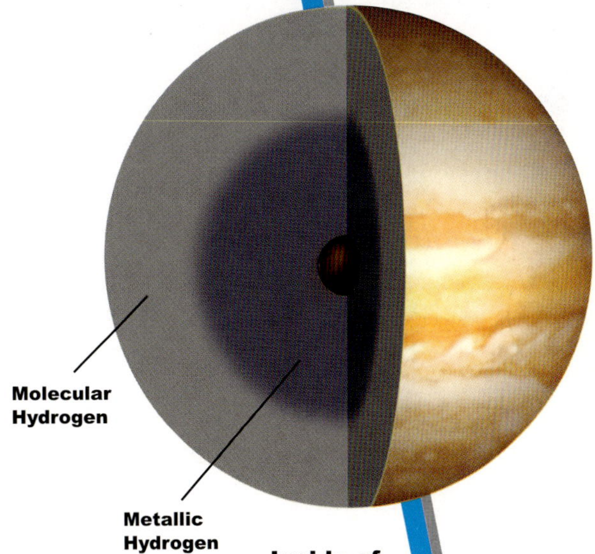

Inside of Jupiter

Great Red Spot

The Great Red Spot is a giant spinning storm on Jupiter that resembles a hurricane. It is brick-red to light brown in colour and is seen around 22° south of its equator. The spot has been observed by astronomers for more than 300 years.

Planet Jupiter

Moons of Jupiter

Jupiter has 62 known moons. The four largest moons—Io, Europa, Ganymede and Callisto were discovered by Galileo Galilei in the year 1610. Ganymede is the largest moon in the solar system with a diameter of 5,232 kilometres. Io, the third largest moon of Jupiter, is the most volcanically active object in the solar system.

Galilean Moons

Ring of Jupiter

Jupiter's Ring

Jupiter has one ring. It is made up mostly of dust particles. The ring is divided into three major components—the main ring, the halo and the faint gossamer ring.

Saturn

The planet Saturn is surrounded by seven thin, flat rings around the equator. Saturn is the sixth planet from the Sun. Saturn is the largest planet after Jupiter and has a diameter of about 1,20,536 kilometres. It completes one rotation in about 10 hours, 39 minutes and takes around 10,759 Earth days to complete one revolution around the Sun.

Saturn

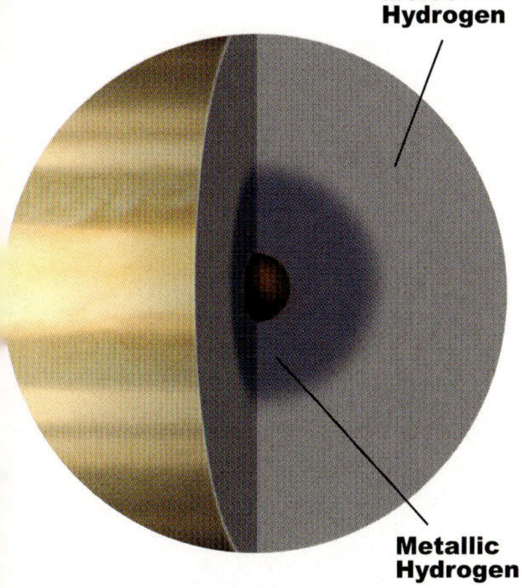

Inside of Saturn

Atmosphere of Saturn

The atmosphere of Saturn is made up of 93 percent molecular hydrogen and the rest helium, with traces of other substances like ice of ammonia, ice of methane and water ice. Saturn has cloud bands in its atmosphere that look pale orange and faded. This colour is because of the presence of large amount of sulphur in its atmosphere.

Surface Features of Saturn

Saturn is the most massive planet after Jupiter. The inner core of the planet is hot and solid. It is made up of iron and rocky material. The core is surrounded by the outer core, which is made up of ammonia, methane and water. The outer core has a layer of thick liquid hydrogen and helium around it.

Rings of Saturn

The rings consist of thousands of narrow ringlets made up of billions of pieces of ice and rock. The rings of Saturn were discovered by Galileo in 1610. The rings make it one of the most beautiful bodies of the solar system.

Rings of Saturn

Moons of Saturn

Saturn has 60 known moons. The first moon to be discovered was Titan. It was discovered by Christiaan Huygens in the year 1655. Jean-Dominique Cassini discovered the next four—Lapetus, Rhea, Dione and Mimas, between 1671 and 1684.

Saturn with Its Moons

Did You Know?

Saturn is the least dense of all planets in the solar system. If one could find a big enough ocean to put Saturn in, it would float.

Titan

Titan is the largest of all the moons of Saturn and the second largest moon in the solar system. Titan is the only moon in the solar system that has a planet-like atmosphere.

Uranus

Uranus is the seventh planet from the Sun. It is the third largest planet in the solar system and has a diameter of about 51,118 kilometres. The planet was discovered by astronomer Sir William Herschel in 1781. It is about 15 times as massive as Earth. Uranus takes 84 Earth years to complete a revolution around the Sun and around 17 hours and 14 minutes to complete one rotation.

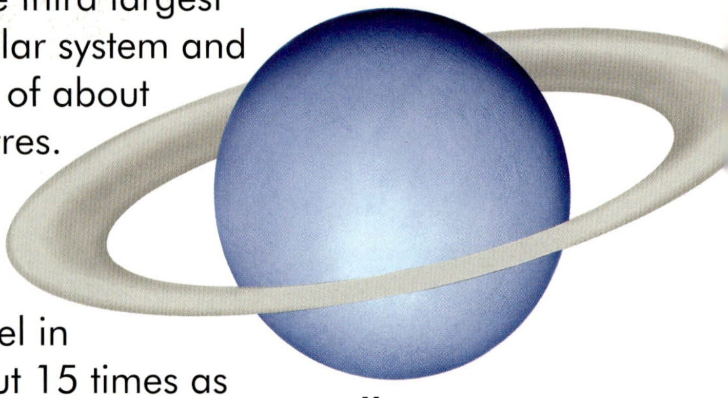

Uranus

Atmosphere of Uranus

Uranus has a very deep atmosphere. The boundary between the atmosphere and the liquid interior of the planet is not very well defined. The atmosphere is composed of 83 per cent hydrogen, 5 per cent helium, 2 per cent methane and traces of hydrocarbons like acetylene. Traces of ammonia and water are also present.

Surface of Uranus

Uranus is a gaseous planet composed of various gases and ice. It has no solid surface at all. The interior of the planet is composed of heavier elements and rocky materials.

Blue-green Colour of Uranus

Blue-green Colour

Methane is one of the constituents of the atmosphere of Uranus. As sunlight is reflected from Uranus' cloud tops, it passes back through the layer of methane in the planet's atmosphere. Methane absorbs the red portion of the light, allowing the blue portion to pass through. This results in the blue-green colour of the planet.

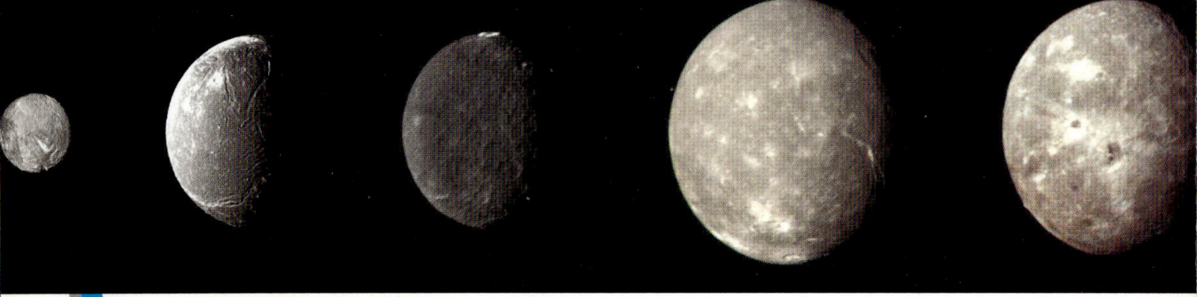

Moons of Uranus

Moons of Uranus

Uranus has 27 known moons. Unlike other satellites that are named after Greek and Roman mythological characters, almost all the moons of Uranus are named after Shakespearean characters. Oberon, Titania, Umbriel, Ariel and Miranda are the five major moons. Oberon and Titania are the largest while Miranda is the smallest of them.

Uranus and Its Rings

Rings of Uranus

Uranus has 11 known rings. The rings are made up of rocks and dust and are less extensive than those of Saturn. The band of rings was first observed in 1977. 1986U2R is the innermost and Epsilon is the outermost ring.

Neptune

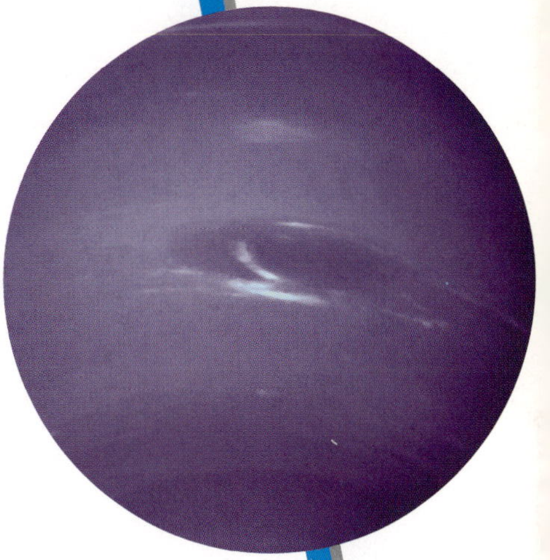
Neptune

Neptune is the eighth planet from the Sun. It is the fourth largest planet in the solar system. It was discovered by Johann Gottfried Galle in 1846. Neptune takes around 16 hours and 7 minutes to complete a rotation on its axis. The planet takes 165 Earth years, that is, about 60,225 Earth days to revolve around the Sun.

Atmosphere of Neptune

The atmosphere of Neptune is made up principally of hydrogen (74 per cent), helium (25 per cent) and methane (1 per cent). The presence of methane gives it a blue colour. The planet has striped clouds and is extremely windy. The planet also experiences great storms.

Surface of Neptune

Neptune is a giant gaseous planet. As such, it doesn't have a solid surface. The interior of Neptune is presumed to be rocky with an icy mantle topped by a deep layer of liquid hydrogen. The interior is unusually hot with increasing temperatures and pressures.

Moons of Neptune

Neptune has 13 known moons. Triton is the largest moon with a diameter of about 2,689.6 kilometres. It is the coldest object in the solar system. Unlike other moons, Triton rotates in the opposite direction to that of Neptune. The other 12 moons of Neptune are Nereid, Despina, Galatea, Larissa, Naiad, Proteus, Thalassa, Halimede, Psamathe, Sao, Laomedeia and Neso.

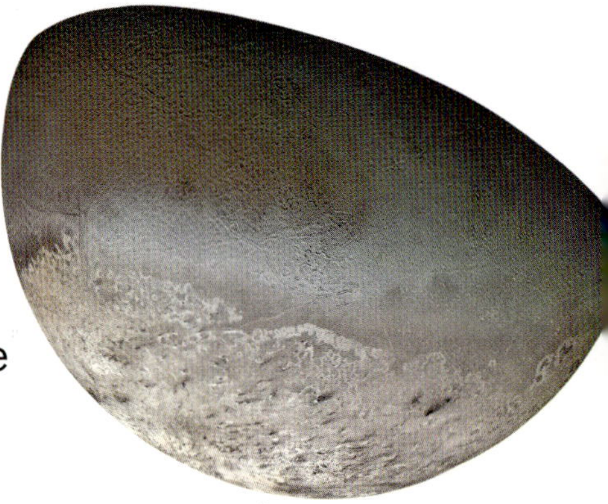

Triton

Rings of Neptune

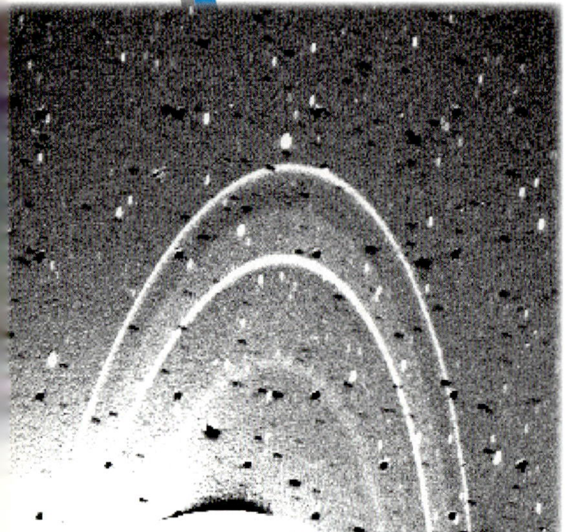

Rings of Neptune

Neptune has six faint rings. These rings were discovered by NASA's Voyager 2 in 1989. The rings are of varying thickness and are made of rocks and dust. The outermost ring is Adams Ring. It has three distinct arcs. They are named Liberty, Equality and Fraternity.

Great Dark Spot

Neptune is the windiest planet in the solar system. The Great Dark Spot is a great storm in the southern atmosphere of Neptune discovered by Voyager 2 in 1989.

Great Dark Spot

Kuiper Belt

Kuiper Belt is a region beyond Neptune. It was named after Gerard Kuiper who proposed its existence in 1951. The belt is a disc shaped region of icy debris. It is at a distance of 7.36 kilometres from the Sun. Scientists believe that most comets originate in this belt.

Kuiper Belt

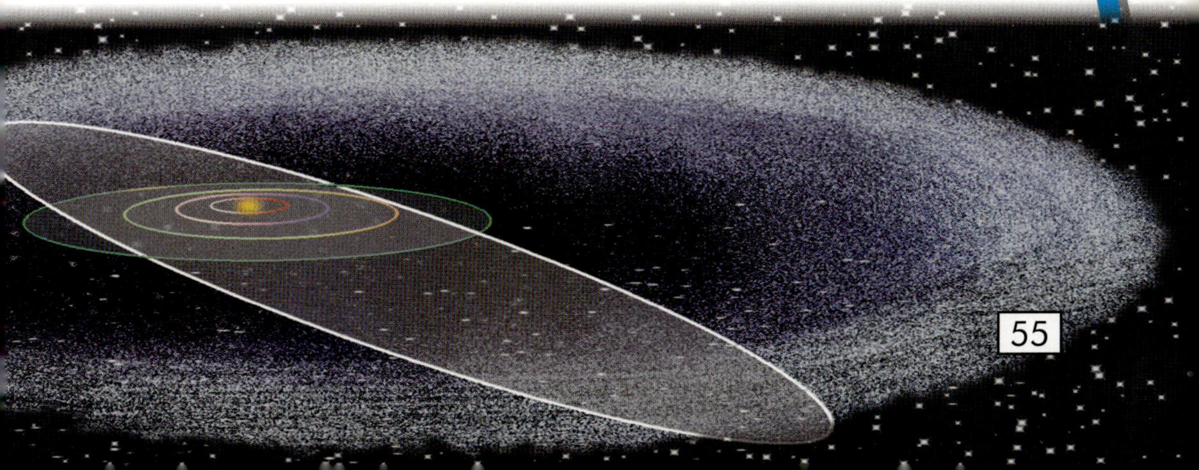

Asteroids

Asteroids

Asteroids are small rocky bodies that resemble planets. Asteroids orbit the Sun like all planets. They are also known as minor planets or planetoids.

Asteroid Belt

Most asteroids are found in a region known as the asteroid belt between the orbits of Mars and Jupiter.

Asteroids in Our Solar System

Astronomers believe that there are over 50,000 asteroids in the solar system. Most of them are found in the asteroid belt. Some are also found between the orbits of Mars and Earth.

Formation of Asteroids

Asteroids are believed to be planetary material that never came together to form planets. The four largest known asteroids are spherical or ball-shaped like Earth. They are called planetoids. Some asteroids are almost as big as some of the moons in our solar system.

Moons of Asteroids

Moon of an Asteroid

Many asteroids revolve around other asteroids. An asteroid that revolves around another asteroid is known as the moon of that asteroid. These asteroids are known as binary asteroids. Some asteroids have moons that are as large as the asteroid itself. Such asteroids are known as double asteroids.

Meteoroids

Meteoroids are smaller than asteroids. They are small pieces of metallic debris. Most of them are even smaller than a pebble. Most meteoroids burn up when they enter the Earth's atmosphere.

Meteor

Meteor

A meteor is a meteoroid that enters the Earth's atmosphere and burns up because of friction. It is commonly known as 'shooting star' or 'falling star' and appears as bright streaks of light in the night sky with a glowing trail.

Meteorites

Meteorites are meteors that reach the Earth's surface. Some of them burn in the atmosphere and some fall as rocks and dust.

Composition of Meteorites

Most meteorites are made up of iron and nickel. They originate from the metallic cores of planets, planetoids or supernova explosions. There are some meteorites that are completely made of stone. They are the most common type of meteorite.

Fireballs

Fireballs are extremely bright meteors. They are sometimes followed by bright trails of light that last for a few minutes.

Fireball

Comets

Comets are small extraterrestrial objects made of ice and dust. They look like stars with a long tail trailing behind. Millions of comets move around the solar system. Most comets are too small and can be seen only through a telescope. Some comets become visible to the naked eye when they pass close by the Sun.

Comet

Structure of Comets

Comets have a solid core surrounded by an atmosphere called the coma and a nucleus. They also have one or two tails. The nucleus, composed of ice and dust, is surrounded by the coma. The coma is a cloud of dust. The nucleus and the coma combine to form the head.

Orbits of Comets

The orbits of comets often extend out of the reaches of the solar system. They often go out of the solar system and come back after thousands of years.

Comet Halley

Halley's Comet orbits the Sun and takes 76 years to complete one orbit. Therefore, it is seen from the Earth after every 76 years.

Meteor Showers

Comets are often responsible for meteor showers. Meteor showers often occur on Earth when the planet passes through the orbit of a comet.

Comet with a Long Tail

Eclipse

Eclipses are astronomical events or effects. Eclipses occur when either the Moon or the Earth blocks out the Sun's rays thereby creating shadows on either the Moon or the Earth.

Total Solar Eclipse

Penumbra and Umbra

Penumbra is the outer and the lighter part of the shadow around the celestial object. The light source is partially blocked in the penumbral region and forms a partial shadow. Umbra is the central and darker part of the shadow. The light source is completely blocked by the celestial object in the umbra.

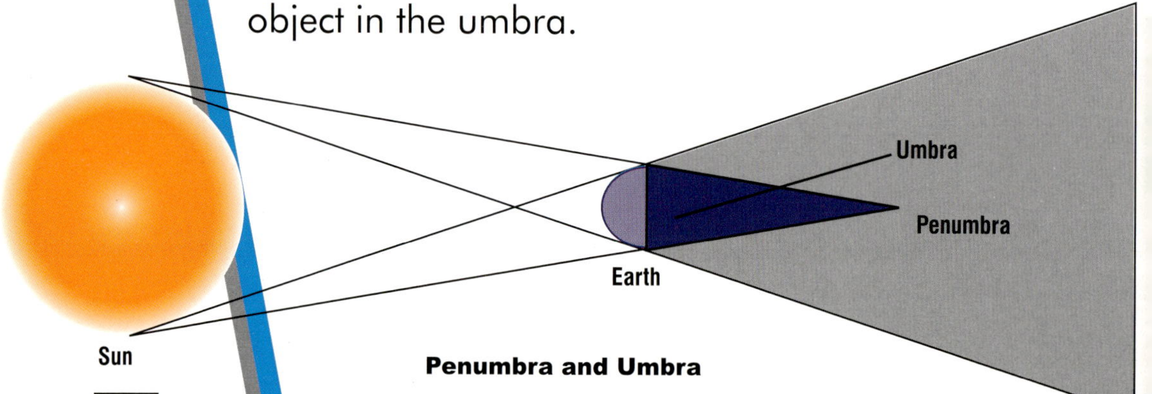

Penumbra and Umbra

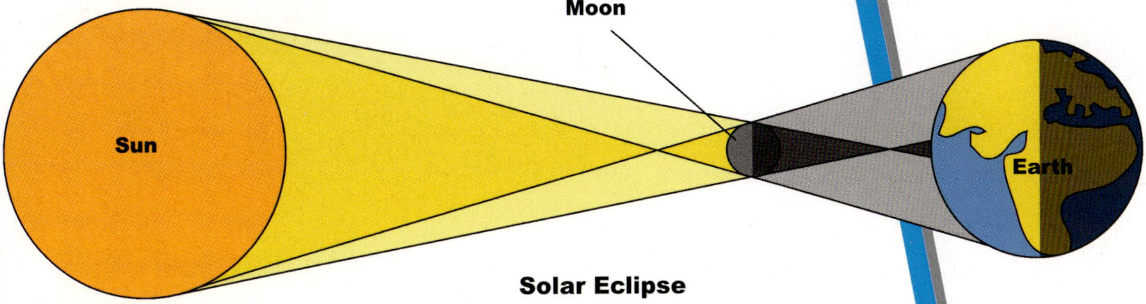

Solar Eclipse

Solar Eclipse

In a solar eclipse, the Moon, the Earth and the Sun all line up with the Moon in the middle. The Moon temporarily blocks the light from the Sun casting a shadow on the Earth.

Features of Solar Eclipse

Solar eclipse can be total or partial. It occurs twice a year during new moon phases. Solar eclipses can last a maximum of 7 minutes and 4 seconds.

Diamond Ring

A diamond ring is the last flash of sunlight from behind the Moon before the beginning and end of totality during a total solar eclipse.

Diamond Ring

Lunar Eclipse

Lunar Eclipse

A lunar eclipse occurs when the Earth comes between the Sun and the Moon blocking the Sun's light. During this period, the Earth's shadow falls on the Moon making it temporarily invisible from the Earth.

Moon During Lunar Eclipse

Features of Lunar Eclipse

Lunar eclipse takes place during the full Moon phase and generally lasts longer than solar eclipses.

Astronomy

Astronomy is the scientific study of the Universe and celestial objects (Sun, planets, comets, galaxies, etc.). Astronomers over the ages have studied the origin, evolution, composition, motions, relative positions and sizes of various objects in the universe.

First Observatory

The first known observatory was built by the Mayans. It was called 'caracol'. The Greeks followed the Egyptians in studying astronomy. They also established many schools to study astronomy.

Astronomical Observatory

NASA

The National Aeronautics and Space Administration, or NASA, is a United States federal agency established in 1958 by President Dwight D. Eisenhower. NASA has its headquarters in Washington D.C., USA. It is responsible for providing technologies for space aviation. It performs test flights and missions and co-ordinates space exploration.

Find

Can you find out the difference between astronomy and astrology?

Radar Astronomy

Radar astronomy is a branch of astronomy that deals with the imaging of nearby astronomical objects. It observes the celestial objects by reflecting microwaves of the objects to be studied and analysing the echoes. Radar astronomy has been used to study the surface features and rotational periods of various planets in the solar system.

Telescopes

Telescope

Telescopes are optical instruments used to magnify and observe distant objects. A telescope gathers light and other radiation and brings it to a focus so that it can be analysed.

Invention of Telescope

The telescope was invented in the 1600s by Hans Lippershey, a spectacle maker from Holland. Galileo was the first person to use the telescope for astronomical observations.

Hubble Space Telescope

Hubble Space Telescope

The Hubble Space Telescope is an optical telescope that orbits the Earth. It was launched by NASA in 1990. The telescope has discovered many galaxies and has shown scientists the various stages of evolution of galaxies. One of the most significant revelations of the Hubble Telescope is the age of the universe. It has estimated that the universe is around 13-14 billion years old.

Astronomers

Astronomers are scientists who study astronomy and contribute to our knowledge of the Universe. Modern astronomers now use a charge-coupled device (CCD) camera and radio telescopes to study the sky. They spend relatively little time using telescopes and spend most of their time in analysing the data.

Aristotle

Aristotle was an early Greek thinker. He believed that the Universe was finite and spherical. According to him, the Universe was centred on the Earth in a perfect circle.

Nicolaus Copernicus

Nicolaus Copernicus was a Polish astronomer and mathematician. Copernicus was the first astronomer to propose that the Sun, not the Earth, was at the centre of the universe and all other planets revolved around it. He also stated that the Earth rotates on its axis once a day and revolves around the Sun once a year.

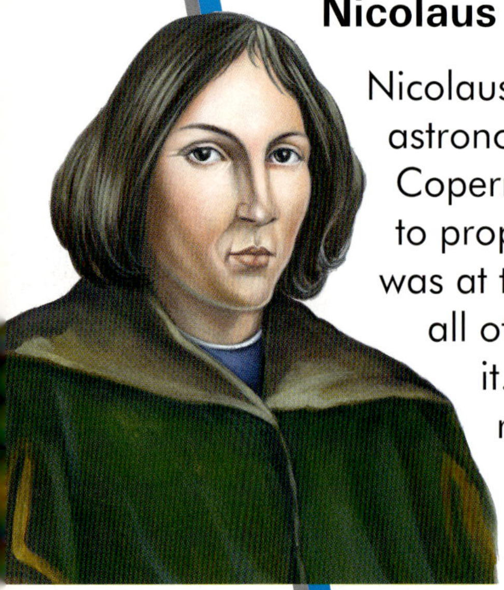

Nicolaus Copernicus

Albert Einstein

Albert Einstein was a physicist. The modern description of the Universe is entirely based on Einstein's theory of gravity that is also known as the general theory of relativity.

Albert Einstein

Galileo Galilei

Galileo Galilei

Galileo Galilei was an Italian scientist, astronomer and philosopher. He made the first astronomical telescope and made many astronomical discoveries. These included mountains and valleys on the surface of the Moon, sunspots, the four largest moons of the planet Jupiter and the phases of the planet Venus.

Stephen Hawking

Stephen Hawking is a British theoretical physicist. Hawking has worked on the basic laws that govern the Universe. He has proved that the Universe does not have an edge or boundary in imaginary time. He has also discovered that black holes probably emit radiation and would gradually evaporate and disappear.

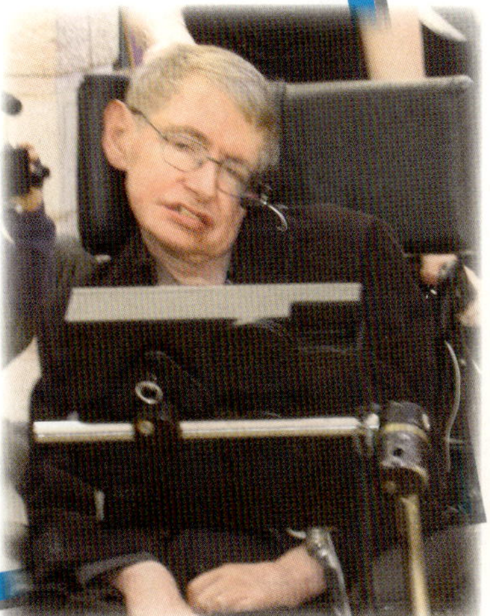

Stephen Hawking

Astronaut in Space

Astronauts

An astronaut or cosmonaut is a person who commands, pilots or serves as a crew member in a spacecraft. Astronauts are trained for space travel in spaceflight programmes. During the training programme, the astronauts learn to control the flight simulator in the shuttle. They are trained about weightlessness or zero gravity.

First Man in Space

On April 12, 1961, Yuri A. Gagarin became the first human to go to space on board Vostok 1. His flight lasted for 108 minutes during which he went around the Earth once. After him many others have also gone into space like Sally Kristen Ride, John Glenn, Kalpana Chawla and Sunita Williams.

Yuri Gagarin

First on the Moon

Neil A. Armstrong was the first person to set foot on the Moon on July 20, 1969. He was the commander of the Apollo II moon landing mission. After him, many others also went to moon like Edwin Aldrin, etc.

Neil Armstrong

Kalpana Chawla

Kalpana Chawla was Indian-born woman and the second person of Indian origin to fly to space in 1998. Kalpana Chawla was aboard 'Columbia' on the ill-fated STS-107 mission.

Kalpana Chawla

Sunita Williams

Sunita Williams

Sunita Williams holds three records for female space travellers – longest space flight (195 days), number of space walks (tour) and total time spent on space walks (29 hours 17 minutes).

Visits to Other Celestial Bodies

The Moon is the only celestial body in the Universe that humans have visited.

Space Shuttle

A space shuttle carries people and cargo into space. Space shuttles can also carry various types of equipment, spacecraft, etc. They also enable the astronauts to service and repair satellites and observatories in space.

Space Shuttle

Gravity Is Zero in Space

Gravity in Space

Many people mistakenly think that there is no gravity in space. In fact, space has extremely low gravity, i.e., about 0.000001 per cent of the Earth's gravity. Therefore, it is said that space has zero gravity or more accurately micro-gravity. Due to micro-gravity, objects are in a state of free-fall and are said to be 'weightless'.

Names of the Space Shuttle Orbiters

The National Aeronautics and Space Administration (NASA) named its space shuttle orbiters Enterprise, Columbia, Discovery, Atlantis and Challenger after famous sea vessels.

> **Find**
>
> Can you find out the names of the Indian astronauts who have gone into space?

Space Shuttle Enterprise

Space Shuttle Enterprise was the first space shuttle orbiter. It was built as a test vehicle and was not equipped for space flight.

Space Shuttle Enterprise

Space Shuttle Columbia

Space Shuttle Columbia was the first space shuttle orbiter to fly into the orbit of the Earth. It was launched on April 12, 1981 from Kennedy Space Centre. During the STS-9 mission in 1983, the shuttle was used to carry Spacelab. Another important achievement of the orbiter was the successful deployment of the Chandra X-ray Observatory in July 1999.

Space Shuttle Columbia

Space Shuttle Discovery

Space Shuttle Discovery

Space Shuttle Discovery was launched for the first time on August 30, 1984. The shuttle was used to deploy three communication satellites on its first mission. Some of its milestones include the deployment of the Hubble Space Telescope (HST) in 1990 and the Upper Atmosphere Research Satellite in 1991.

Space Shuttle Challenger

Space Shuttle Challenger was launched for the first time on April 4, 1983. The shuttle accomplished nine successful missions before it exploded on January 28, 1986 killing all seven astronauts on board, 73 seconds after launch.

Space Shuttle Challenger

Space Shuttle Atlantis

Space Shuttle Atlantis (OV-104) was launched for the first time on October 3, 1985. The Atlantis has carried out several important voyages, including the Galileo planetary explorer mission in 1989 and the deployment of the Arthur Holley Compton Gamma Ray Observatory in 1991.

Space Shuttle Atlantis

Measurement Units

Measurement is the calculation of the size or amount of a quantity. The global standard of units is the International System of Units (SI units). It is used widely around the world. Astronomical distances are measured in three main units: astronomical unit, light year and parsec. One astronomical unit (AU) is equal to about 93 million miles. One light year is equal to 95,00,00,00,00,000 kilometres, and 1 parsec (pc) is the distance equal to 3.26 light years.

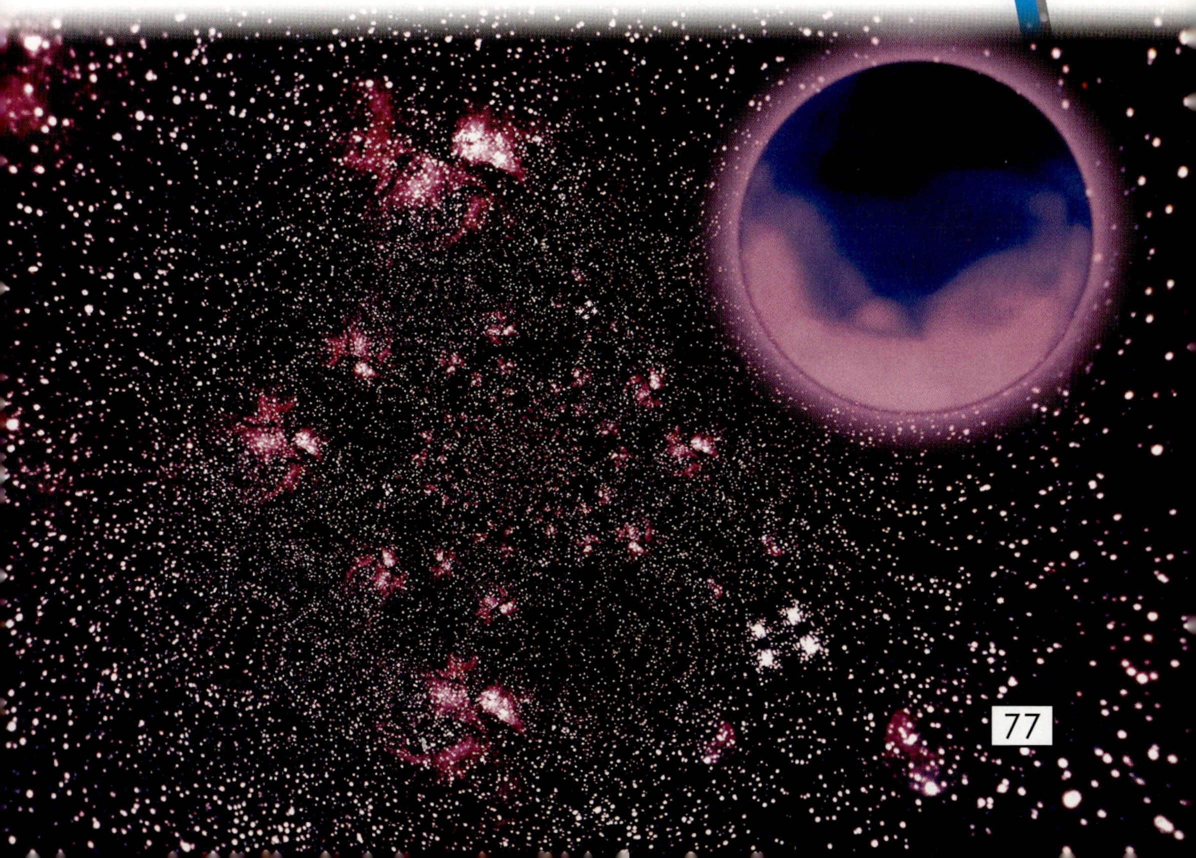

Astronomical Unit

Astronomical unit (AU or au) is the mean distance between the Earth and the Sun. However, it is actually slightly less than that as it is based on the radius of a circular orbit.

Examples of distance in AU:

- Distance of the Earth from Sun is 1.00 ± 0.02 AU
- Distance of the Moon from the Earth is 0.0026 ± 0.0001 AU
- Distance of Mars from the Sun is 1.52 ± 0.14 AU

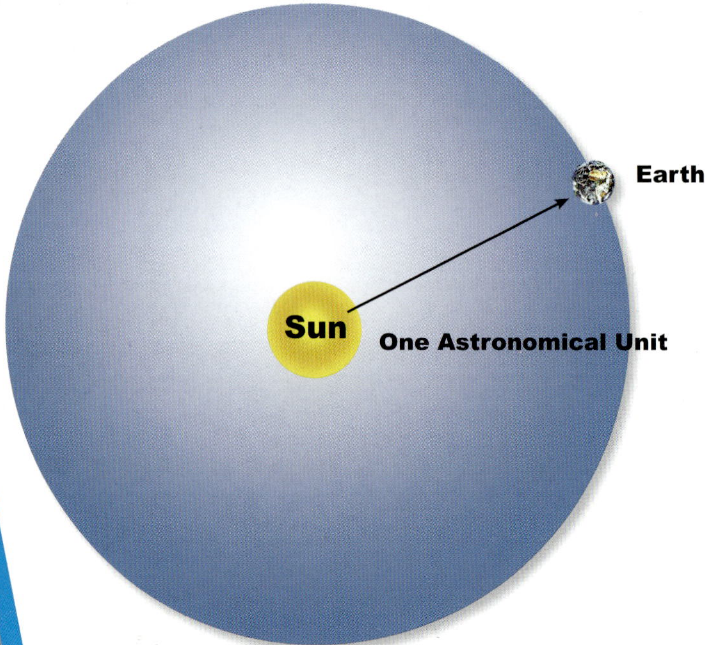

Astronomical Unit (Mean Distance between the Earth and the Sun)

Parsec

Parsec stands for parallax of one arc second. It is the distance at which an object in space forms a definition of 1 arc second from Earth. It is the oldest method of measuring the distance of astronomical objects from Earth. It is equal to 3.262 light years.

Light Year

A light year is another measuring unit for astronomical distances. The distance travelled by a light particle in one year at a constant velocity of 3,00,000 km/sec is known as light year. One light year is equal to 94,61,33,33,76,000 kilometres. It is equal to about 63,240 AU.

Herbert Hall Turner

Herbert Hall Turner was an English astronomer and seismologist. He coined the term 'parsec' and named the dwarf planet Pluto. He modified several measurements so that they could be used for astronomical purposes.

Herbert Hall Turner

Index